YEAR C

Every Day of Advent and Christmas

A Book of Activities for Children

Advent Calendar Included!

TO THE ADULT

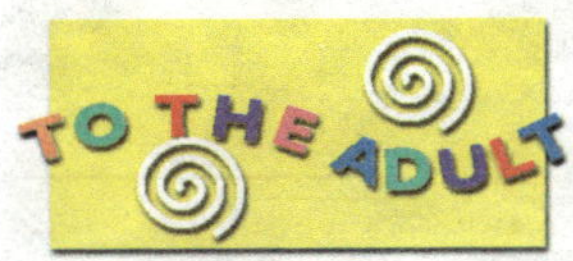

Where activities are lectionary based, the Sunday Scripture is noted in the green banner. Citations are from the *Lectionary for Masses with Children.*

Younger children may need help with

- The Jesse Tree, pages 2-4
- The Story of Advent and Christmas, p. 6
- Game of Love, p. 14
- The Story of the Epiphany, p. 32

Please provide children with

- crayons, markers, or colored pencils
- pencil and eraser
- glue or paste
- scissors
- construction paper
- tracing paper
- materials for the Jesse Tree

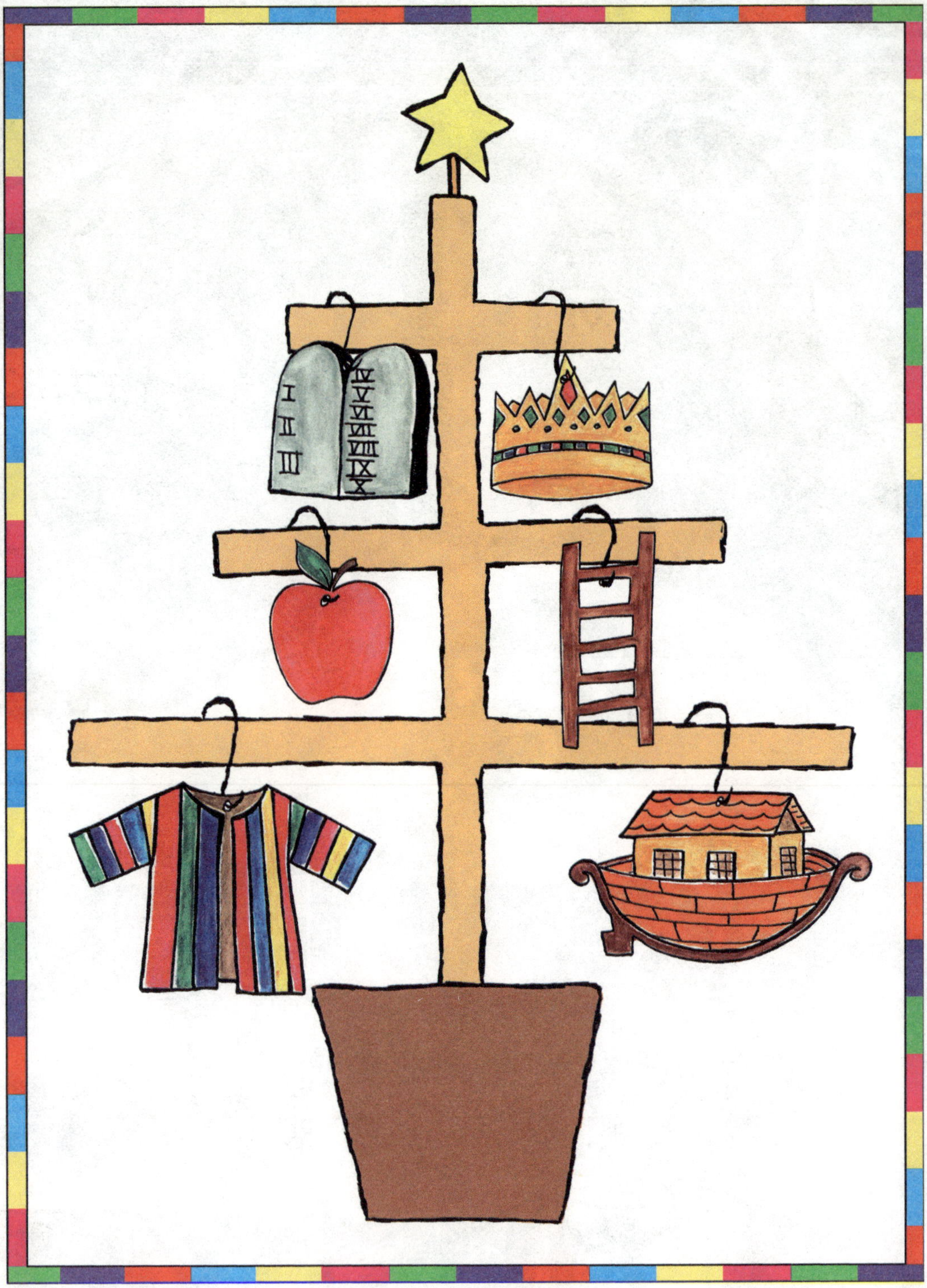

The Jesse Tree: Our Ancestors in Faith

The ornaments on the Jesse Tree show us some important people in Christ's family tree. Cut out a Jesse Tree from construction paper, or plant an actual tree branch in a can filled with sand. Each week the class or family can remember the events of salvation history by creating and adding ornaments to the tree and talking about ancestors of our faith. Cut out, decorate, and hang on your Jesse Tree the ornaments on page 3, as well as any others you would like to design.

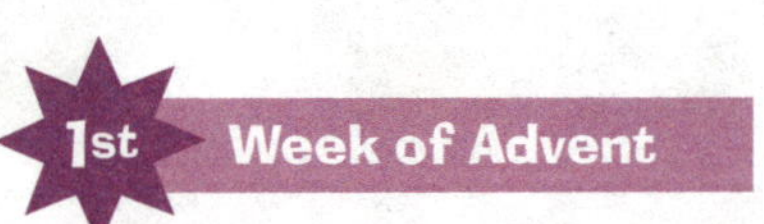

Ornaments for Your Jesse Tree

Wreath—The First Week of Advent

To find some words to an ancient Advent song, use the same color for all the panes in the stained glass that have a dot in them. Use your favorite stained-glass colors for the other panes. If you want your Advent wreath to look like the one in church, color three candles purple and one rose or pink. Or use your favorite colors.

people of Israel

king

slavery

heal the sick

set the people free

Advent

Jesus

Christmas

The Story of Advent and Christmas

A long time ago, the  were waiting for a  to be born. This  would save the  from . The  would  and  from their enemies. The  waited a very long time for their good  to be born.

During the four weeks of , we too wait for the birth of that , who is .  did  and  from the  of doing wrong. We celebrate the birth of  on  day.

How to Read This Rebus Story

Use the key at the left to help with the story.

Dear Jesus,

Amen

Dear Jesus

Without Jesus, we would not have Christmas. Take a minute to write a prayer or letter to Jesus. It can be about anything you choose.

Wreath—The Second Week of Advent

As in week one, color the panes with the dots to find the Advent message. We are a week closer now to our celebration of the birth of Jesus at Christmas. As you color your wreath this week, say a prayer for someone you love.

Saint Juan Diego

Feast Day — December 9

Saint Juan Diego ✶ Juan Diego, a Native American man, was made a saint in 2002. He is a special patron or helper for all people who live in the Americas. Our Lady of Guadalupe appeared to him and left him her picture on his cloak. As you color the picture on this page, say a little prayer to Saint Juan Diego for someone you know who needs help. Then read the story of Saint Juan Diego on page 10. His feast day is December 9.

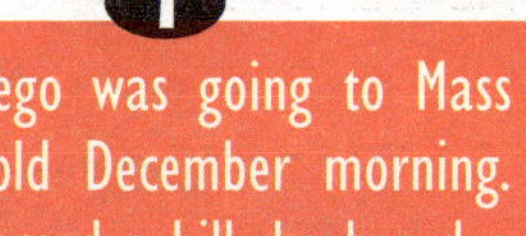

Juan Diego was going to Mass on a cold December morning. As he passed a hill, he heard a sweet voice call his name.

He saw a beautiful woman who told him she wanted the bishop to build a church on the hill.

Juan Diego went to the bishop, who asked for a sign and sent Juan away.

The next time Juan saw the beautiful woman, she told him to go to the top of the hill, pick the roses he found there, and take them to the bishop.

Somehow there were roses on the hilltop, so Juan picked them and carried the roses in his cloak. When he showed them to the bishop, everyone saw a picture of the beautiful woman on his cloak.

The bishop believed Juan's story and ordered a church built on the hill. We call the beautiful woman Our Lady of Guadalupe. Her feast is December 12. She is the patroness of the Americas.

Roses in December

Read box number one and fiind the picture it matches. Draw a line connecting them. Do the same for box two and so on. Now read the whole story in the boxes in order from one to six.

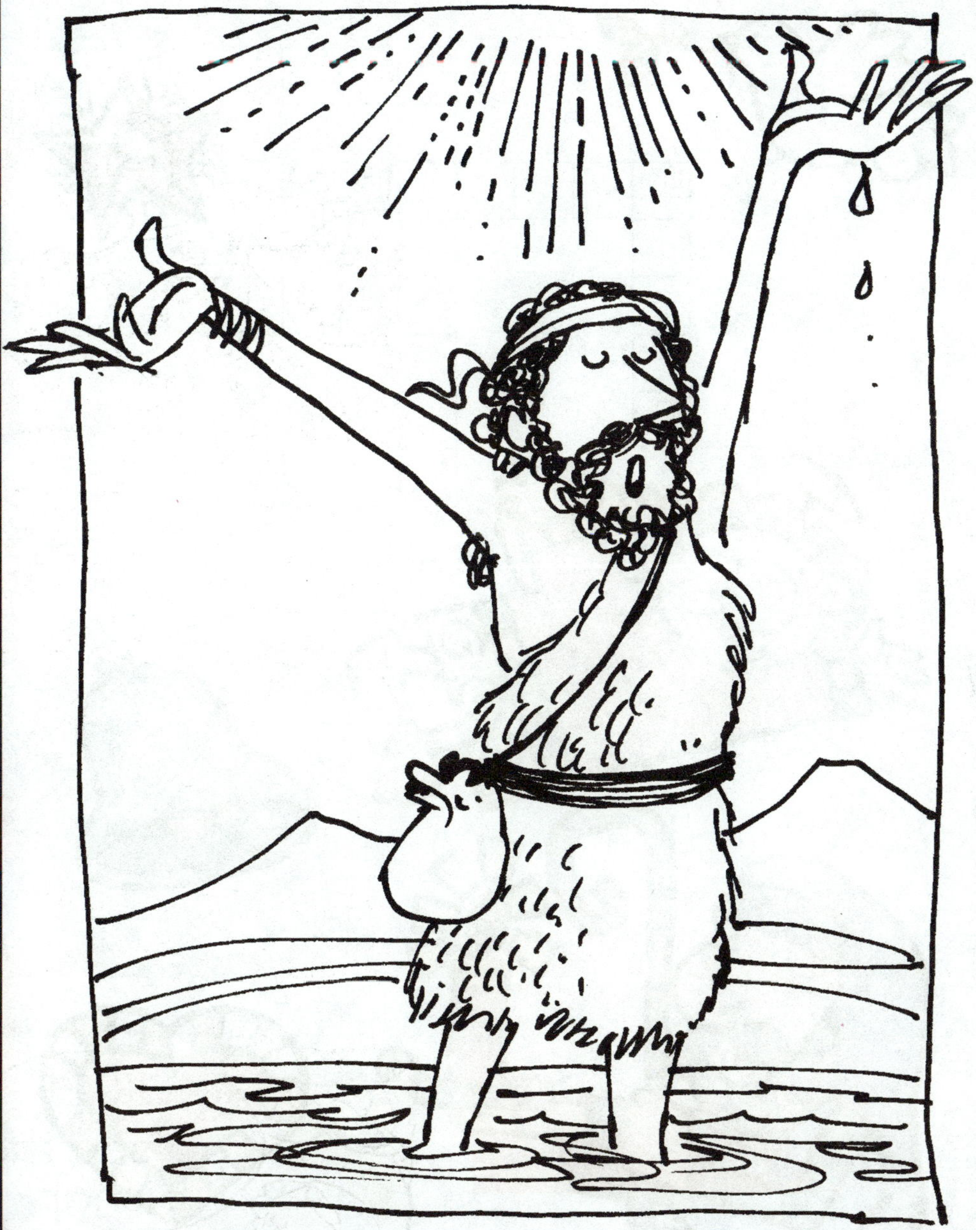

Prepare the Way of the Lord!

John the Baptist

Many people went out into the desert to hear John the Baptist, who was Jesus' cousin. As you color this picture, see what John had to say to the people, and think about how you, too, can prepare for the coming of Jesus.

Luke 3:1-6

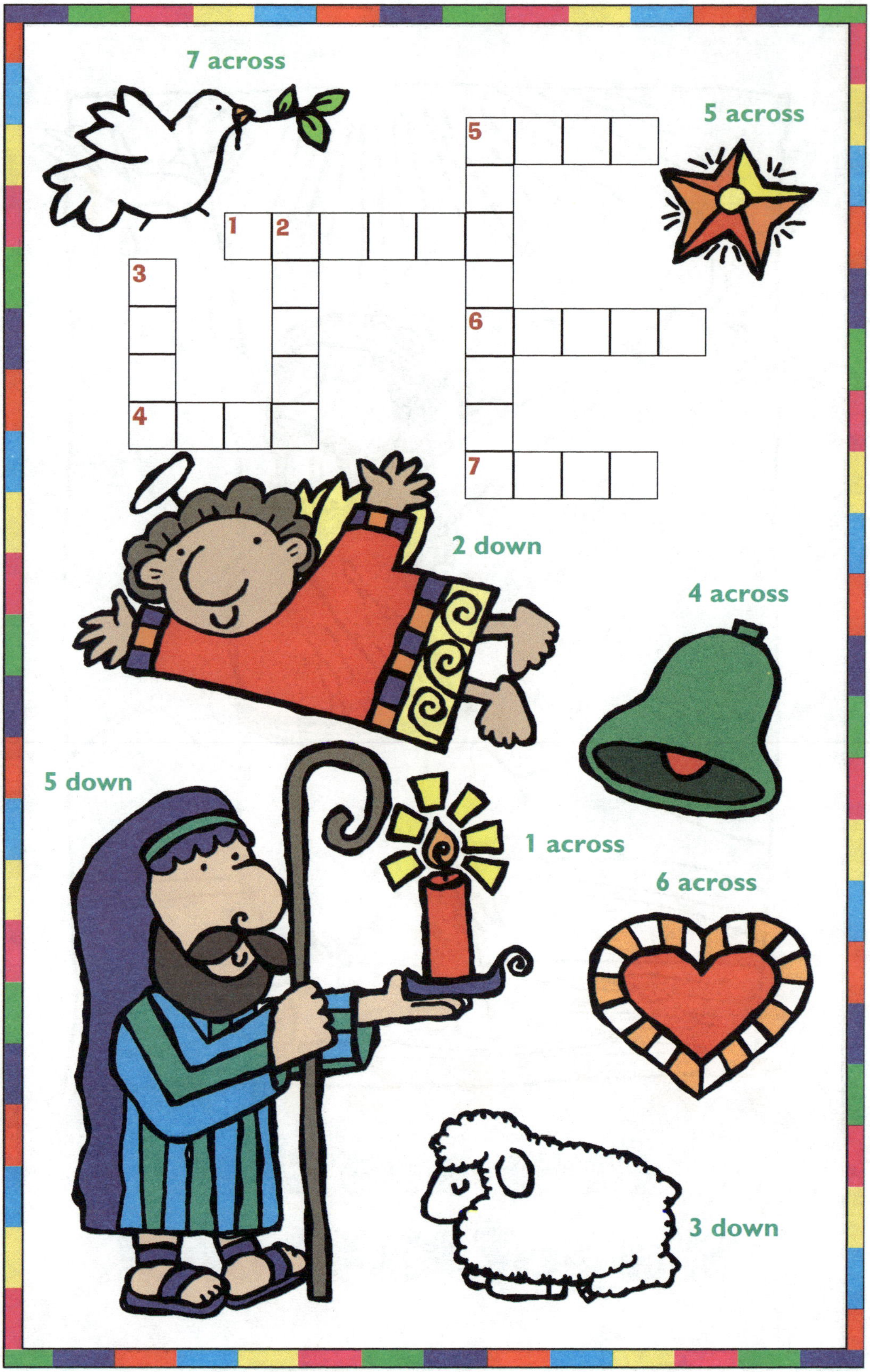

7 across

5 across

2 down

4 across

5 down

1 across

6 across

3 down

Crossword Puzzle

During Advent, you see, hear, and feel many things. Look at the picture clues and solve the crossword puzzle.

C	S	P	E	C	A	O	I
C	H	B	B	H	D	Z	X
B	E	R	N	R	V	O	L
E	P	U	I	I	E	S	T
L	H	V	L	S	N	B	C
D	E	H	J	T	T	K	G
N	R	L	N	M	Q	O	M
A	D	S	T	A	R	L	A
C	X	Z	M	S	G	T	N
C	M	L	P	Q	H	S	G
G	A	L	E	G	N	A	E
B	R	S	C	D	Z	U	R
A	Y	J	O	S	E	P	H

Can You Find Them?

Find the 10 words listed below. Be sure to look carefully. They go in different directions.

☐ ADVENT ☐ CHRIST ☐ CHRISTMAS ☐ CANDLE ☐ STAR

☐ MANGER ☐ ANGEL ☐ SHEPHERD ☐ JOSEPH ☐ MARY

Go to the

bird

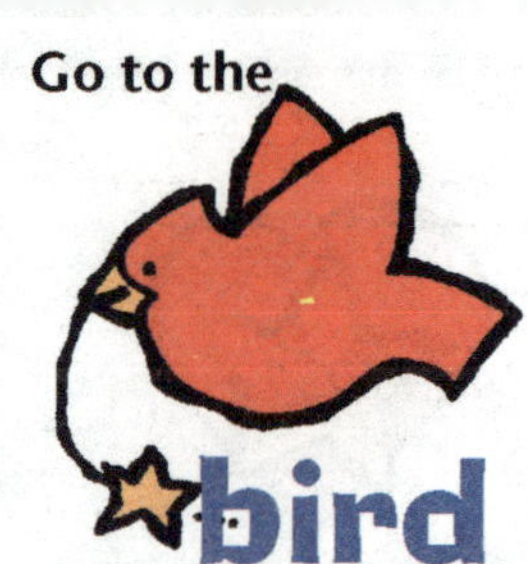

Go to the

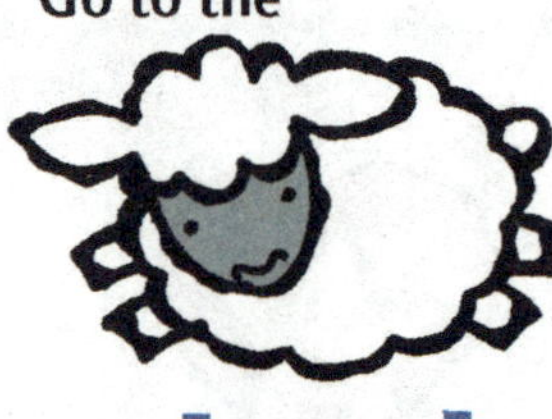

lamb

Go to the

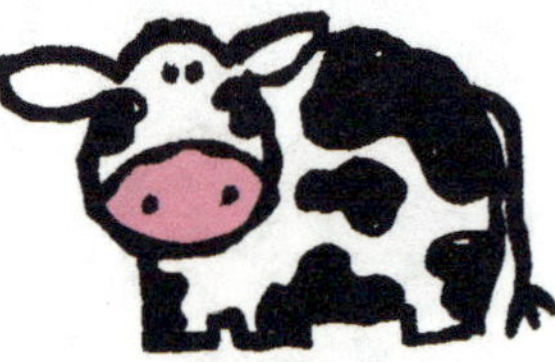

cow

Go to the

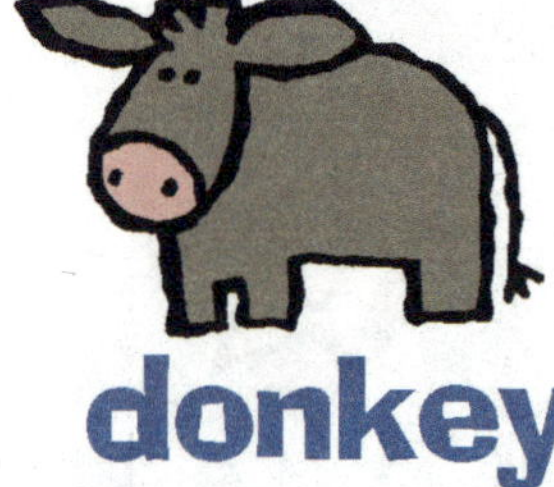

donkey

Go to the

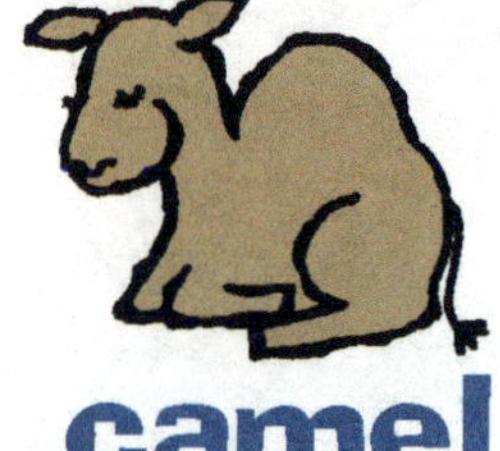

camel

Go to

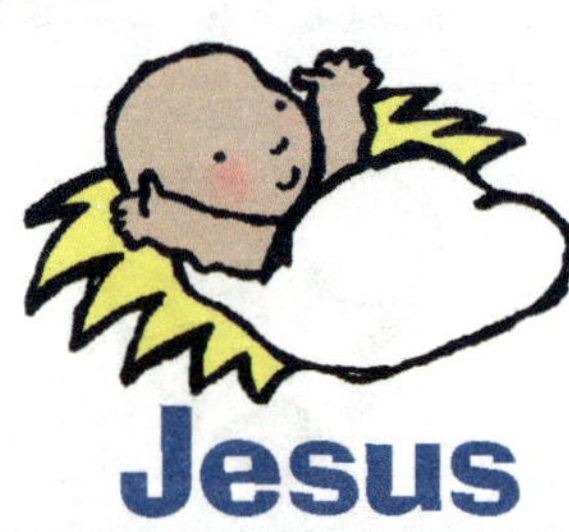

Jesus

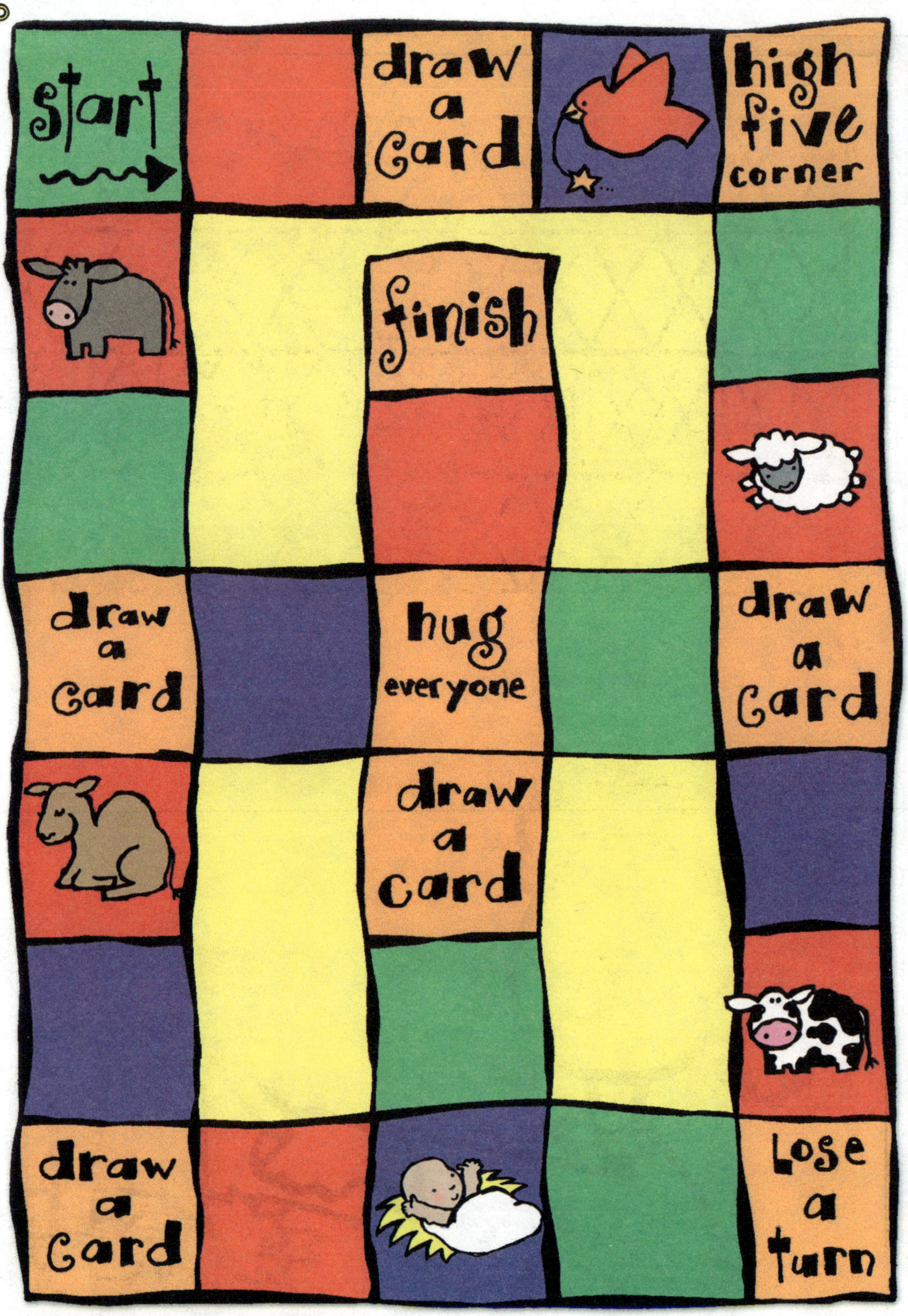
start
draw a card
high five corner
finish
draw a card
hug everyone
draw a card
draw a card
draw a card
lose a turn

Place cards here

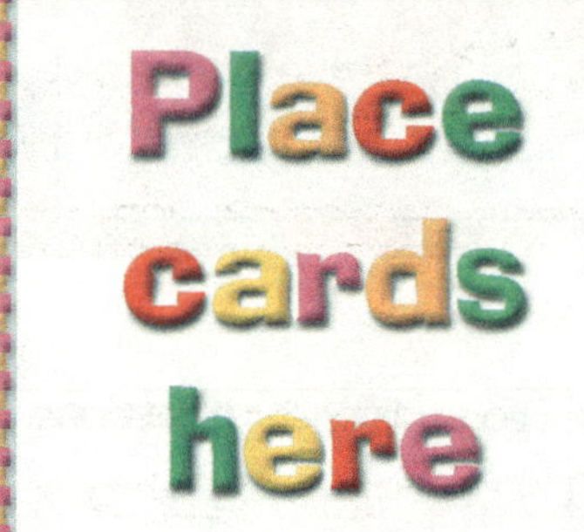

Game of Love

Cut out and shuffle the cards on the left side of this page. Place them upside down in the square to the left. Flip a coin to move. "Heads" you move two spaces, "tails" you move one space. Follow the instructions on the card or on the board space. After you draw a card, return it to the bottom of the deck, and continue playing until someone reaches the end.

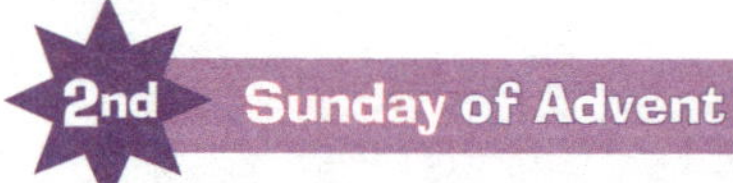

Wreath—Third Week of Advent

Even though we are still waiting for Jesus' coming, we rejoice today because Jesus is near. As you color the third candle the rose color of rejoicing, say a prayer for someone who brings joy into your life. Color the panes with the dots to find the Advent message.

Countdown to Christmas Calendar
Fill in your calendar! Here are 24 squares, one for each day before Christmas.
Starting with December 1, place the first square in the appropriate box. Use the calendar to help you count down to Jesus' birthday. This can be a family or individual activity.
1
5
9
10
11
15
16
17
20
21
22

2
3
4
6
7
8
12
13
14
18
19
23
24
Merry
Christmas!

Find the Message

Saint Paul taught his friends and us how to follow Jesus. To decode the message, match the letter in the top row of the key to the letter underneath it. Fill in each blank with the new letter. Now you can see what Saint Paul said.

Make Your Own Ornaments

Trace the angel and wreath onto tracing paper. Then trace them onto construction paper, cut them out, and decorate them on both sides. Ask an adult to help you with the hook. When you're finished, hang them on your tree or give them as gifts. Color and cut out and use the little gift tags in the margin for presents.

Merry
Christmas

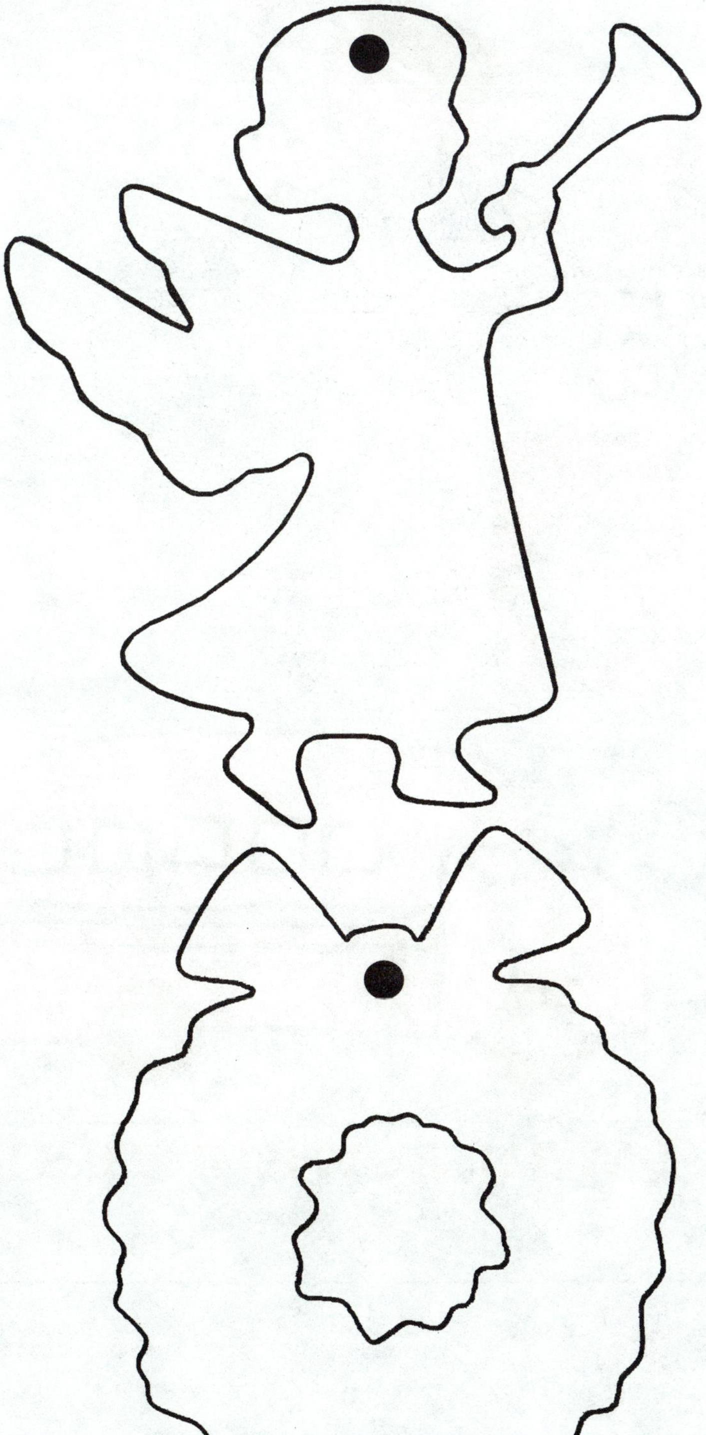

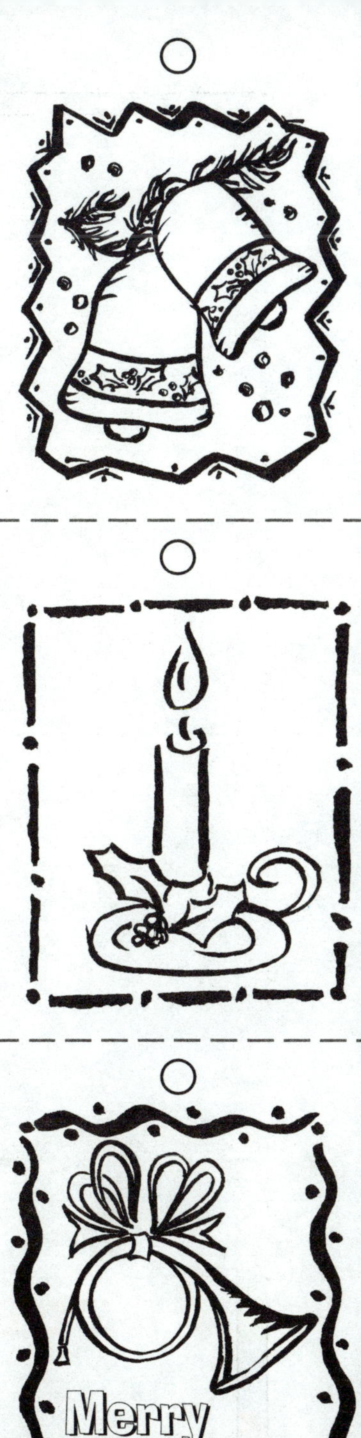

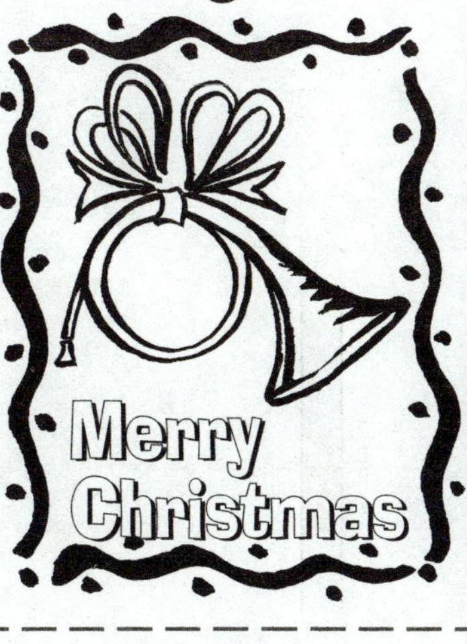

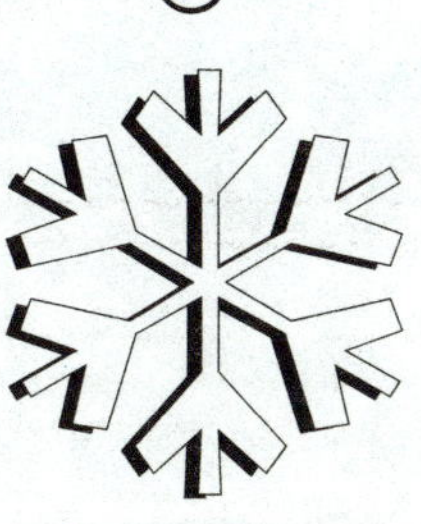

Do Not
Open Until
Christmas!

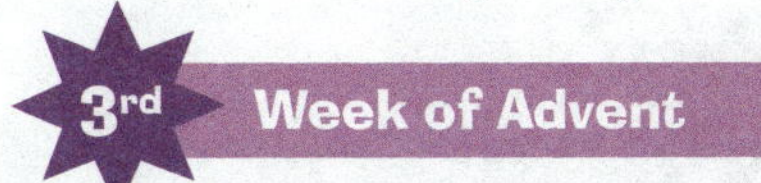

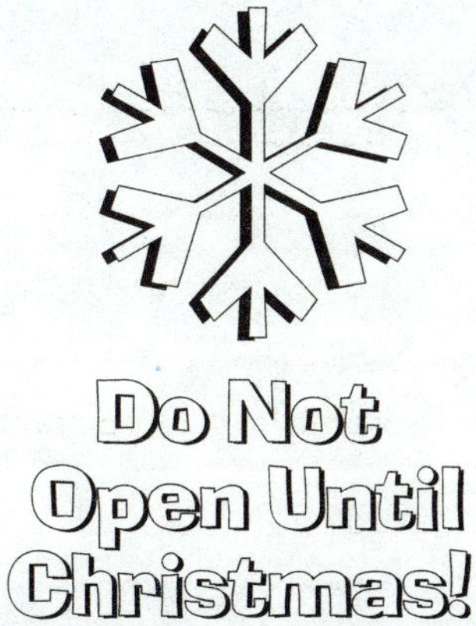

To:

From:

To:

From:

To:

From:

To:

From:

– t

– tamp

+

– B = ___ ___ ___ ___

What's This?

Whose birth do we celebrate on Christmas? Solve the rebus puzzle to find out.

Which One Is Different?

Draw lines joining matching pairs of stars to find the one that is different from all the rest.

Wreath—Fourth Week of Advent

Color the panes with the dots to find the Advent message. Everywhere there are signs of getting ready for Christmas. As you color this last wreath of Advent, say this prayer: *Dear Jesus, Make my heart ready for you on Christmas. Amen*

Mary's Song of Praise

Unscramble the letters and fill in the blanks with the words Mary spoke with Elizabeth. Then color the picture.

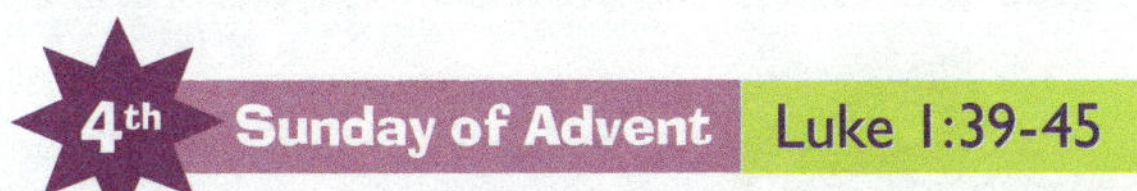

The Reason for the Seasons

Hold the picture above about six inches from your eyes. It looks like a jumble of dots. Now look at the picture again from a few feet away. Do you see a difference? Suddenly the picture has a meaning: it is the face of Christ, who is the reason for the seasons.

My Gift to You

Make your own card. Trace this Christmas card onto a piece of paper. Decorate and fold it in half. Write a special Advent or Christmas message inside.

Mary/María

Joseph/José

shepherd/pastor

burro/burro

luminary/luminaria

soldier/soldado

Las Posadas (A Place to Call Home)

For nine days before Christmas, Latinos celebrate Las Posadas by dressing up and coming together to pray, sing, and rejoice in Jesus' birth as our Savior. Joseph and the sheperds, soldiers, farmers, and workers go from house to house looking

farmer/granjero

musician/musico

singer/cantante

piñata/piñata

girl/muchacha

boy/muchacho

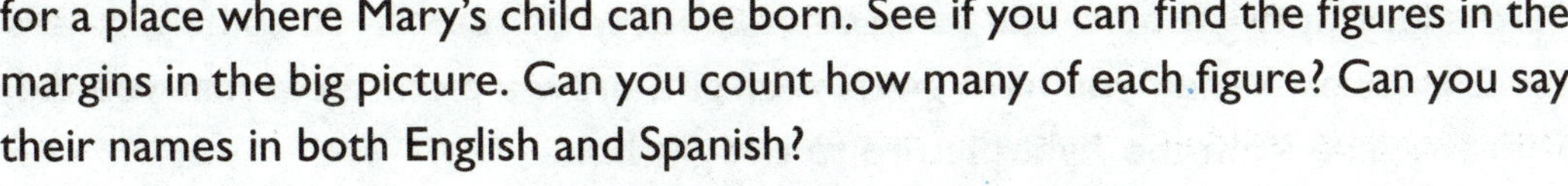

for a place where Mary's child can be born. See if you can find the figures in the margins in the big picture. Can you count how many of each figure? Can you say their names in both English and Spanish?

A Gift for Others

Here is an empty gift box. Talk to an adult about what you can do to help others this Christmas. When you have given your gift, draw a picture of what you did, or draw a line from the right picture to the gift box.

The Birth of Jesus

Cut on the dotted lines and paste the missing people or objects that belong in this picture.

A B C

D E F

(E) ___ ___ ___ ___ ___ SSUEJ

(C) ___ ___ ___ ___ ___ SIFTG

(B) ___ ___ ___ ___ ABML

(F) ___ ___ ___ ___ MRYA

(A) ___ ___ ___ ___ SATR

(D) ___ ___ ___ ___ ___ GNAEL

Christmas Symbols

We see many symbols during Christmas. Unscramble the words above. Then match the picture to the correct word.

El Día de los Santos Reyes (The Day of the Three Kings)

In Mexico, children do not receive presents from Santa on Christmas. But don't worry! The Three Kings bring the gifts on Epiphany. Miguel has put his shoe and a note on his windowsill, asking for his favorite toy. Help the Three Kings find Miguel. Beginning with the yellow star, use your pencil to join the stars whose points are touching. Happy Epiphany, Miguel! (¡Feliz dia de los santos reyes, Miguel!)

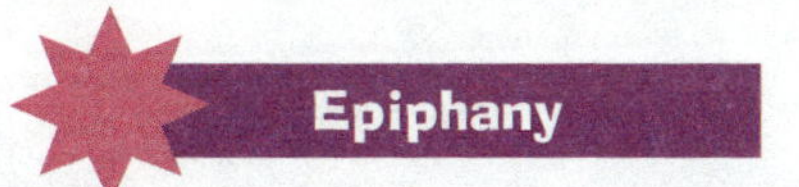

Rebus Instructions

Use the key below to help with the story.

Jesus

Wise Men

Star

King Herod

Gifts

Jesus, Mary, and Joseph

The Story of the Epiphany

At the time  was born, three  saw a  . The knew that the  would lead them to a new king, so the  followed the  . When the  came to Jerusalem, they asked  where to find the new king,  .  told the to go to Bethlehem where the new king would be born, but 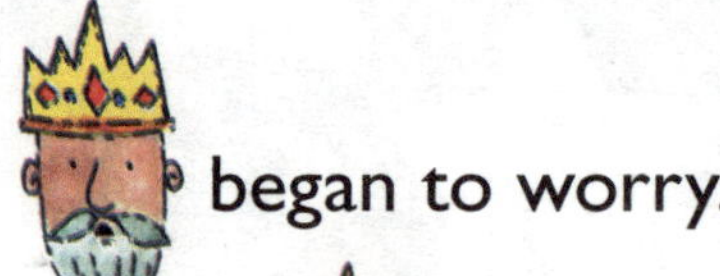 began to worry.  didn't want a new king to take his place. So  told the  to come back and tell him about  . wanted to do away with  . When the  found , they knelt down and offered  their  . That night, God spoke to the  in a dream and told them not to return to , so the  went home another way.

Liguori
One Liguori Drive
Liguori MO 63057-9999

Art and design: Wendy Barnes, Jodi Hendrickson, Christine Kraus, and Chris Sharp.

ISBN 978-0-7648-1541-6
50000
9 780764 815416